RECAST

James McLardy

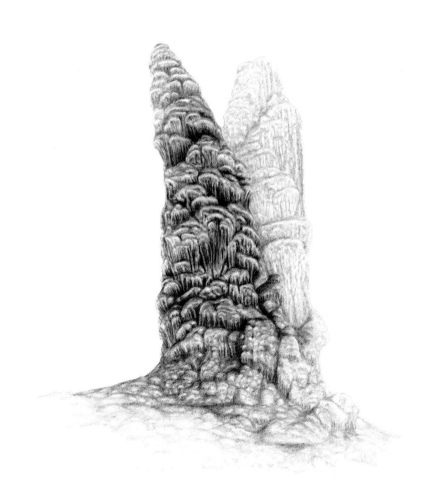

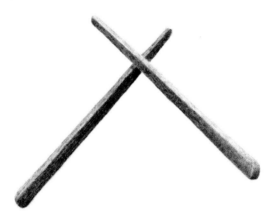

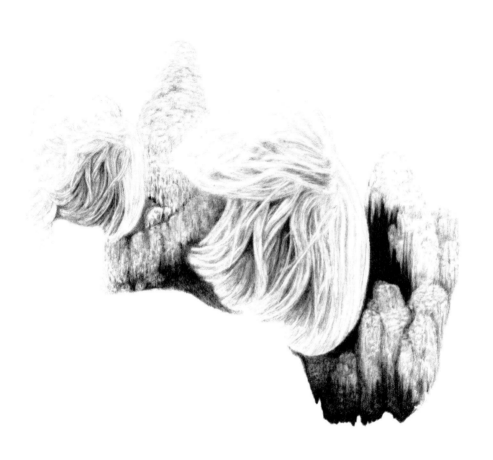

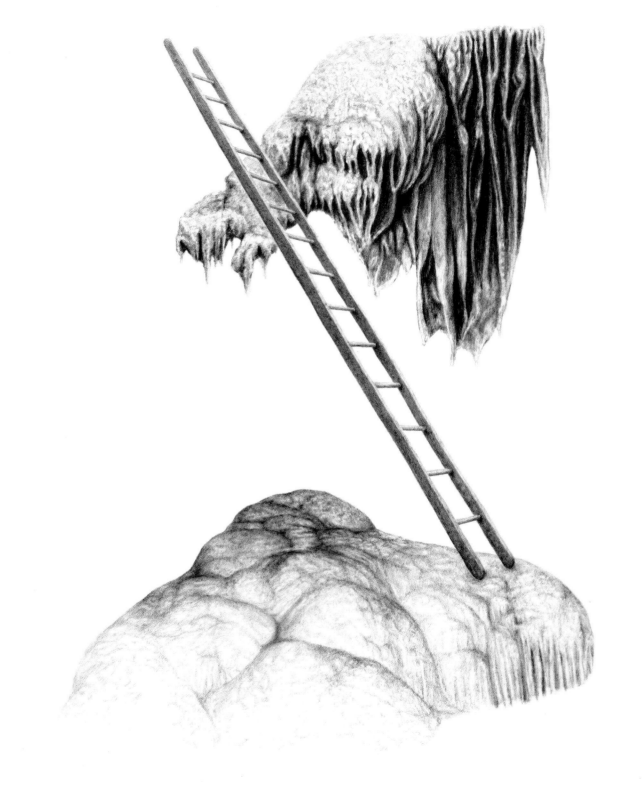

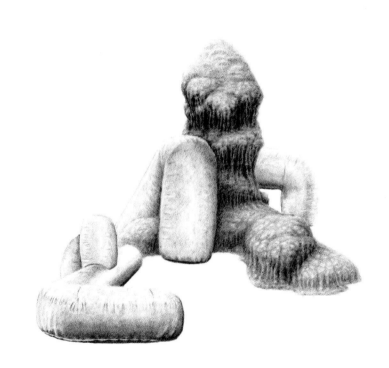

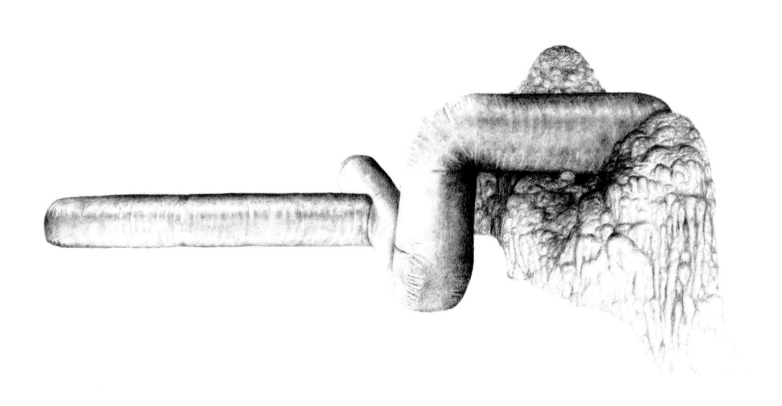

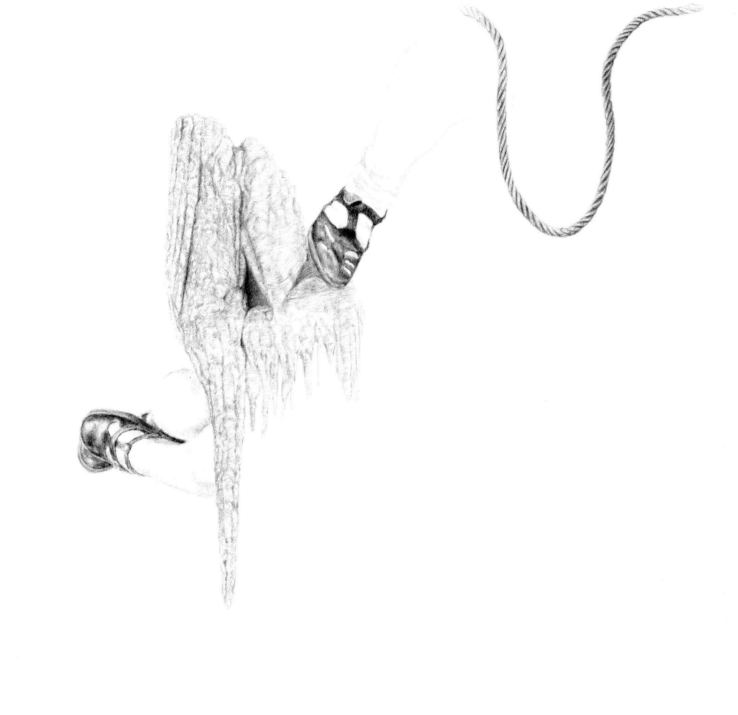

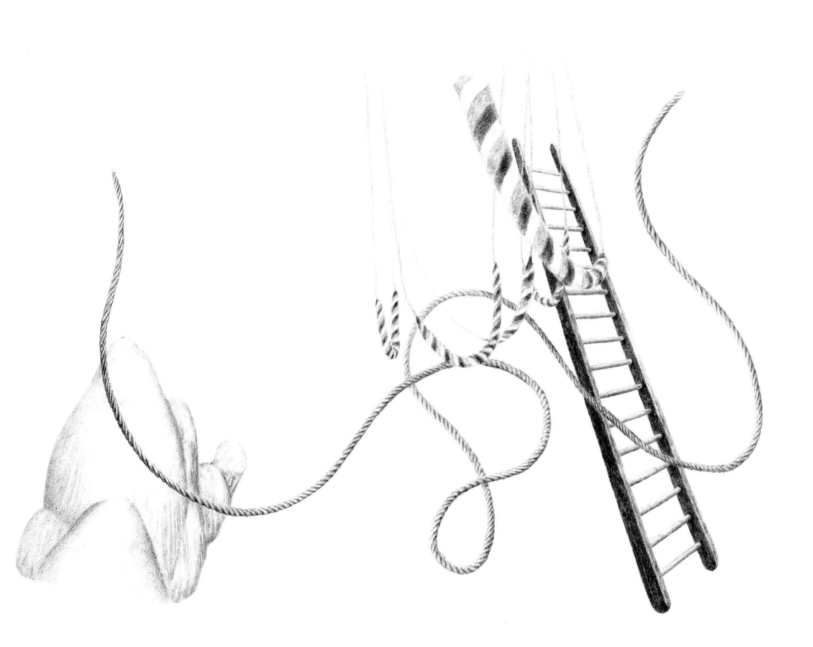

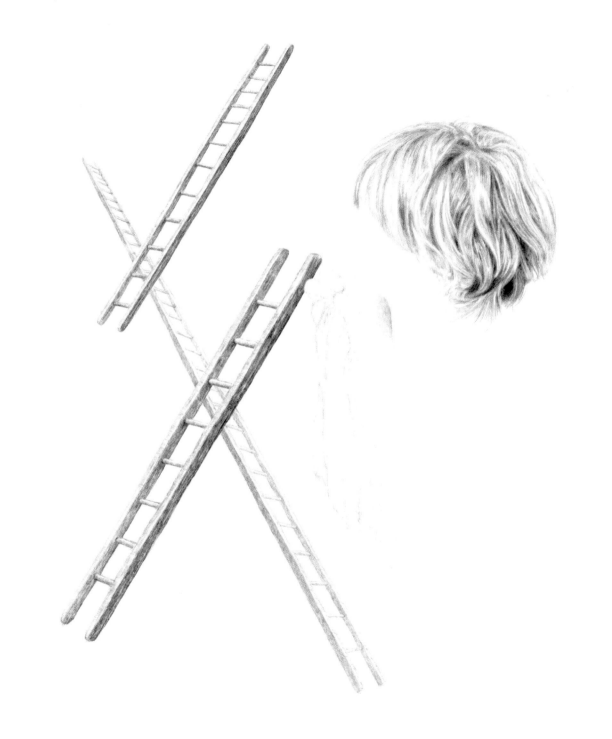

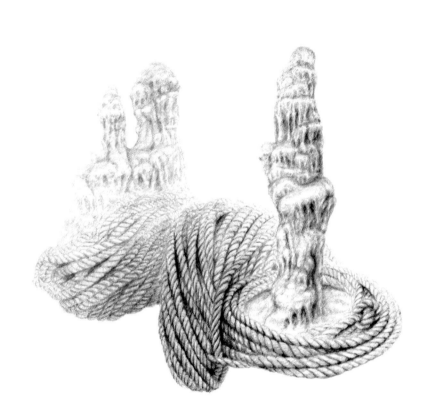

He had commanded a wall to be made round him, and procured an iron chain, twenty cubits long, he fastened one end of it to a great stone, and the other to his right foot, so that he could not, if he wished, leave those bounds. There he lived, continually picturing heaven to himself, and forcing himself to complete things which are above the heavens; for the iron bond did not check the flight of his thoughts.